Amy Lynn Durham

CREATE
MAGIC
AT
WORK

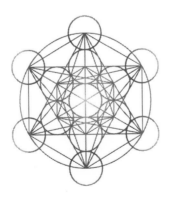

Practical tools to ignite
human connection

ILLUSTRATIONS BY MARYBEL MARTIN

TABLE OF
CONTENTS

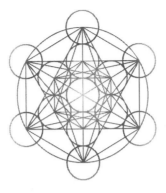

CREATE MAGIC AT WORK:
PRACTICAL TOOLS TO IGNITE
HUMAN CONNECTION

© 2020 Amy Lynn Durham

Published by
Amy Lynn Durham
amydurhamexecutivecoaching.com

Illustrations by
Marybel Martin
marybelmartin.com

Cover and interior design by
Chad W. Beckerman
chadwbeckerman.com

Paperback ISBN: 978-1-09831-451-4

PREFACE

"What's your company's culture like?"

HOW MANY TIMES HAVE YOU BEEN ASKED that question? What is your answer? Do you even know? There are hundreds of books on the topic, and yet many companies fail to truly distinguish themselves with an extraordinary company culture.

Your culture could be hard to define if you don't know where to start. I've seen executive after executive gather in meeting rooms and spend hours discussing what culture means to them, debating their vision or mission, etc. Unfortunately, oftentimes none of the high-level consideration that goes into defining the culture ends up trickling down in any material way to the frontline employees who are literally the face and real culture of your company.

Creating true company culture comes from bringing different people together, pinpointing their unique skills and celebrating those skills in a way that contributes to the whole of the team. As Oprah Winfrey has said, "People want to be seen, heard, and feel like they matter." Unfortunately, ego gets involved in corporate culture time and again, especially at upper-management and executive levels, where some leaders feel they have to be in control or somehow demonstrate that they know more than everyone else. Letting go of that control and admitting you do not know everything can be a scary prospect for some. Deep down as a leader, you may feel as though if you do let go, or show that you actually don't know everything, your employees will think you're not worthy of the title or place that you hold within the organization. However, I've discovered that the exact opposite happens when a leader lets go of that control. For example, some of the most powerful statements I've made as a leader have been:

"I MADE A MISTAKE."

"WHAT ARE YOUR THOUGHTS ON THIS?"

"I'M NOT AN EXPERT ON THIS TOPIC."

"LET'S CALL HANNAH AND GET HER FEEDBACK."

"WE HAVE A PROBLEM THAT NEEDS TO BE SOLVED, AND I DON'T HAVE ALL THE ANSWERS. I'D LIKE EACH INDIVIDUAL TO BRING TWO PROPOSED SOLUTIONS TO OUR MEETING."

Lack of trust is another stumbling block for building a real-life, amazing company culture. This issue can present itself in many ways within an organization, such as an executive who thinks he or she knows better than the masses and micromanages the employees instead of granting them real responsibility and decision-making power, or fear-based management, based on the flawed idea that employees won't be as productive because they aren't worried about keeping their job or striving for more profit at all times.

There are still thousands of companies that use distorted, negative, competitive tactics to pit employees against each other in order to reach their goals. While these companies may have earned the profits or revenue they were striving for at that particular time, what about all of the hidden costs? Were the employees burned out, driving them to leave the company and resulting in large costs in rehiring and retraining? Was mental stress carried into employees' home lives, leading to employees with increased health problems? Was so much animosity created between people that they can no longer collaborate harmoniously?

Think of the alternative: Could the profits have been even higher if there had been healthy competition where everyone contributes to the overall goal and plays a part in its success?

Do you want to be known as a stress reliever or a stress inducer?

Many business leaders are "all about the numbers," watching results on revenue streams constantly. However, they ignore the data, which clearly shows that building a positive company culture through autonomy, flexibility and effectively using people's talents and skills actually increases profitability. This is what I like to call the "Selectively Data-Driven Executive." In a time when people no longer work at one particular company for their entire lives and instead job-hop around, the cost of attrition has a real impact on a company's bottom line.

It is worthwhile to let go of that fear of loss of control, or fear that people won't do the right thing. If you invest in employees' emotional well-being, helping to foster more human connection and elevating emotional intelligence, you will attract the individuals to your organization who are willing to go above and beyond. They will do this because you chose to give them the tools they need to become a better leader and a better person.

Surrounding yourself with unique, talented individuals is the first key to cracking the code in building a phenomenal company culture. And guess what? You are already surrounded with unique, talented individuals most of the time. It just takes getting to know them on a more personal level and realizing what their strengths are and developing those strengths for the benefit of the whole team or company. This handbook is designed to give you practical tools that you can utilize to bring out the unique qualities of your employees and build a truly positive company culture that you are excited about and proud of. These practical tools are also great exercises and modalities that you can utilize during one-on-one sessions with employees or "coachees" if you are an Executive or Life Coach.

SOME GROUND RULES TO PONDER

NEVER SCHEDULE A TEAM-BUILDING EXER-cise or a meeting centered on increasing employee engagement or morale during people's regular time off of work. When you do this, it says to the employee, "We care about you, but not enough to take away your time when we need you working hard for what we pay you." And to make matters worse, you are taking away time from their personal lives. Respect for personal lives and time will gain your employees' loyalty in the long term. When you carve out time during regular business hours to conduct personal growth and development, you are sending a strong message that this is an important part of a thriving business.

*"People will forget what you said. People
will forget what you did. But people will
never forget how you made them feel."*
–MAYA ANGELOU

Utilizing the following exercises and modalities will not only make a positive impact on your bottom line, but will also send ripple effects out into the world because of the progressive differences you make in people's lives. Each of the following exercises and modalities can be incorporated during your regularly-scheduled, in-person meetings, and many can be done virtually. Some methods can simply be scheduled strictly for the team build without any regular business items being discussed. If you do use these exercises/modalities during normal meeting times, I recommend first covering essential business information and initiatives that need to be addressed, and then ending the sessions with a team-build exercise. This way, employees leave with a feeling of positivity and beneficial self-development techniques to make them better leaders when they return to their respective employees. More often than not, they will do a similar team-building exercise with their employees who report to them, and you have created a nice ripple effect in your organization. Incorporating these techniques into one-on-one meetings with your employees or coachees as modalities is a helpful way to facilitate thinking and connecting with each other. This practical guide of real-world items and exercises/modalities will move you from the thinking-and-talking-about-company-culture phase to the action phase. Let's act!

> *"Action has magic, grace*
> *and power in it."*
> –JULIA CAMERON

JOURNALING TOGETHER & WITH A *TWIST*

Every morning we are born again.
What we do today is what matters most. "
–BUDDHA

AMONG THE MANY HEALTH BENEFITS OF JOUR-
naling is alleviating stress. Working to reduce the stress
level of your employees aids in quieting their left brain, the
analytical side, and opening up space for their right brain
to engage in creativity and inspiration. This is when the

true magic happens! You are opening up space for them to build skill sets which cannot be replaced by a computer.

You will be amazed by the gratitude and loyalty your employees will display when you set aside company time to work on personal well-being. Nothing demonstrates caring more than when a leader invests his or her company time in their employees' personal growth. One particular thing to note with the journaling team-build exercise: This is an extremely beneficial tactic to use with men (as are all of the exercises included here). Many boys are taught to suppress their intuition and creativity. But giving those same boys, who are now men, a safe space to express what has been suppressed will aid in emotional balance and help them become better leaders and better men.

If you have some trepidation about trying this exercise with a group of boiler-room mentality individuals, who may think journaling is for the sixteen-year-old teenage girl writing in her diary, just start off the exercise by citing all of the benefits that they will receive by journaling. Who can argue with you when you are offering time to do something that "Reduces stress . . . Improves immune function . . . Keeps memory sharp . . . Boosts mood . . . [and] Strengthens emotional functions," as Kasee Bailey noted in her blog entry "5 Powerful Health Benefits of Journaling."

Here's how to get started:

1. Set time aside at the end of your meeting for your team to spend in quiet-reflection journaling. There are a variety of journal prompt cards available online. (I've included a few of my personal favorites on the Resources page.) They all give specific topics and questions to help inspire journaling. If you have the budget, make it more meaningful by buying each member of your team a journal and pen to use just for this purpose, and hand them out as a gift before you begin. If you have a team name or logo, you might even want to have journals printed with that on the cover.

2. To begin, take out your journal prompt cards and, keeping them face down, go around the room and have each person draw a card. Make sure to stress that, whatever card they choose, its message is specifically meant for them.

3. Give everyone about fifteen minutes of silence to reflect on the topic of the card that they chose, and then write about it in their journals. During that time you can play some peaceful, meditative music.

4. Once everyone is finished, open up the floor

for discussion. Ask for volunteers to share with the group what their topic was and what they wrote in their journal. It is imperative that you do not require everyone to share. Just create a safe space where everyone is offered a chance to have a voice within the group. All teams have certain personality dynamics, and some individuals tend to be more talkative and outspoken compared to others. Always make it a point to recognize the quiet individuals and ask them if they would like to share, but give them respect and reverence if they choose to keep their journaling moment to themselves and opt out of sharing. If you call on someone who is traditionally very quiet and they say they do not want to share, simply say, "No problem. I just wanted to make sure you had a voice and were heard by the group if you wanted the opportunity." Then move on to the next person.

5. End the session when everyone who wants to share has done so. I always let everyone keep the journal prompt card they chose as a memento from the experience.

DARE-TO-DREAM EXERCISE

"The Grass is Greener Right Here."
–DAVID AULT

IF YOU ARE LOOKING FOR A VERSATILE, CREATIVE activity to incorporate into one of your meetings or individually with a coachee (virtual or in person), this exercise is a perfect choice. You can facilitate it for fifteen minutes or up to an hour depending on the number of participants and the amount of sharing you allow. Just the act of visualizing the removal of the perception of what we "have to do" and replacing it with choices results in a huge stress reduction and cultivates feelings of empowerment. Giving someone permission to work on their personal goals while at work builds loyalty, and returns on this time investment will last a lifetime and more.

1. Before beginning this exercise, have every participant shut down all of their electronics so there are no distractions. Dim or turn off the lights in the room. I like to use essential oils in this exercise (as well as in many other exercises). Offer each individual a drop of lavender or a good balancing essential oil in their hands. There are so many to choose from. (I've included some that I recommend on the Resources page).

2. Ask the participant(s) to close their eyes so that they can more easily calm down and get grounded. (Of course if anyone feels uncomfortable doing that, it's not required). Instruct everyone to rub their hands together to activate the oils, then hold their hands in front of their faces, inhaling deeply three times.

3. Next, guide everyone to imagine their life if they never had to work again or earn a paycheck.

Here are a few questions you might ask to help them consider this idea more effectively: "What would that look like? What would you do with the rest of your life? What happens when you release the belief that you have to wake up and earn a paycheck every day to get by? Imagine you have everything you need financially ... now what?"

Spend about three minutes in silence, letting them visualize what their life would look like under these circumstances.

4. Next, restore the lights, ask the participant(s) to open their eyes, and hand them a blank piece of paper and a pen. For the next five to ten minutes have each individual write down a list of five things they would do in their life if they never had to work a day in their life again.

5. When everyone is finished with compiling their lists, open up the group for sharing and discussion. Remember, not everyone is required to share, but everyone is welcome to and will always have a voice if they need to use it. You are just offering psychological safety to share.

6. Now, for the punchline. As the leader or coach, at the end of the meeting you are going to

require each individual to pick at least two items on the list that they are committing to accomplishing right now or within a certain time frame. The reality is most people do have to get up and go to work every day to earn a paycheck. But the reality, also, is if you prioritize your time and goals appropriately, you can accomplish many things that you may think you can't accomplish because you are telling yourself, "I have to work."

In the past when I've moderated this exercise, I have had some really serious, as well as humorous, goals achieved. For example, I saw one person note that they would like to travel to Europe, and the goal was achieved by that summer.

I've seen fitness and health goals written down that they want to achieve; fitness is often something that people who work long hours must sacrifice. But if you can inspire others to dedicate time to their health and wellness, it will pay you back hundreds of times over in sound decision making and positive leadership, not to mention the savings in health costs and losses to the business if, or when, they have to go out on leave for medical or stress issues.

Another employee in this exercise said he wanted to lie on the couch all day and smoke meats in a meat smoker, which gave everyone a good laugh. Fast forward to this employee's birthday, and the team pitched in money and gifted him with a meat smoker. He was extremely touched. It made something fun and humorous impactful and built camaraderie within the group all at the same time. Now, after the exercise, the laughs, and the gift, if an individual on the team needed some extra help, our meat-smoker employee would be more willing to take their call and work together rather than just fending for himself, once again aiding in contributing to the collective success of the company and team.

Remember to have your employees set deadlines as to when they would like to accomplish these "if I never had to work" goals and mark them on their calendar. Follow up in casual conversations with each individual to see how their progress has been. Do not follow up with them as you would for a work task or project. This should not become a stressful task that they have to accomplish.

Revisit this exercise in another six months to a year to help with changing priorities and life events.

INTENTION
SETTING
EXERCISE

"Intention leads to behaviors
which lead to habits which lead to personality
development which leads to destiny."
–JACK KORNFIELD

AIDING A GROUP OR INDIVIDUAL IN SETTING intentions for what they want to bring into their lives, or possibly let go of in their lives, is a very powerful practice. Many times we can get extremely caught up in our day-to-day routines, and we forget to stop, take a step back, and look at ourselves, our businesses, our long-term or even short-term goals with an aerial view. It gives people time to reflect: "What do I really want in my life?" "What do I want to let go of that is no longer serving me?"

This exercise gives your employees permission to take the time to do this. The tool that I like to use with intention-setting exercises is flying wish paper. If you've never heard of it, it is awesome! (I've highlighted my favorite types on the Resources page.) You can also just use journals or sheets of paper for this exercise, but I highly recommend the flying wish paper for the "WOW!" effect.

If you are able to meet with your team in person this is a great exercise to gather everyone around after a meeting or after dinner. I once rented out a bed and breakfast for my team, and we did this intention-setting exercise before everyone went to bed. It was extremely impactful. This will connect your team with each other on a higher level, build psychological safety, and bond everyone together by building empathy and respect for one another.

Hand out a piece of wish paper to every individual and ask them to write two to three intentions, wishes, or goals that they would like to bring into their life. Stress to the group that this is their own personal-growth exercise and the intentions can be either business-related or personal. Once they write their intentions down on the wish paper, ask for volunteers to share their intentions. If it is a smaller group, then everyone should have a chance to share.

Saying these intentions out loud in front of their peers has a powerful effect and helps to bring those intentions into their lives. Be sure to keep an eye on the silent ones in the group. Call on them and ask if they would like to share. But if they opt not to share with the group, respect their space. I've discovered that by doing this you are letting people know that they are seen and can be heard if they choose to be. Make sure not to underestimate the quiet individuals in a group. Some of them are the most deeply impacted by these exercises. I've had many individuals who are more comfortable in a one-on-one setting pull me aside to let me know how inspiring this was and thanked me for the session.

Once everyone has had an opportunity to share, if you are using the wish paper, ask everyone to crinkle up their paper, roll it into a vertical tube, then set it on a little square of cardboard, and light the tip on fire. Everyone can light their wish paper on fire at once, or you can choose to go around the room and have each person share and light theirs one by one. The intentions that were shared burn to the bottom of the board, lift off of the board and fly into the air, sending your intentions off into the universe. It is a very magical thing to witness. People love the feeling of watching and being a part of this.

If you want to delve even deeper with your intention-setting exercises, you can time them with the phases of the moon. The new moon is a great time to set intentions for things that you would like to bring into your life. You can share with everyone that as the moon grows, you can watch your intentions grow. In addition, if you are near the time of a full moon, it is a great time to let go of something that is not serving you in your life.

If you don't care about the moon phases one way or another, have your team pick either something to let go of, or something they want to bring into their life and write it on the paper. Either way, the WOW! effect and impact will be there.

Be prepared to respect whatever may be shared. As a leader or coach, many people look to you as a mentor and someone to look up to. Therefore, things may be shared that are very sacred or personal. I recommend just holding space for that moment in time and then moving on afterward. For example, I performed the flying wish paper exercise with a team around the time of the full moon, and I recommended writing two to three items down that you want to let go of or release in your life. One individual shared with the group that he was going to forgive his parents. He took a deep breath, lit the paper on fire, and we all watched it burn and fly into the air. It was a beautiful moment. Others may share something humorous, such as releasing their anger that their favorite team didn't win in the NBA finals.

Either way, lead the exercise with no judgment, and let everyone share what they wish. The different personalities and the acceptance of where each individual is in their life are what make the world less boring and more fun to partake in.

You can also use this exercise in front of larger crowds, and it has a very profound impact. I once helped the CEO of a large organization let go of a really rough prior year for the company in front of all of his executive leaders. It was extremely cathartic for him to simply write the prior year's number down on wish paper in front of everyone, light the wish paper on fire, watch it burn down then fly up in the air, and, finally, let it all go and move forward to what came next. It was not only healing for himself, but for his team who watched him do it. I was honored to be a part of it.

MORE
THAN
S'MORES

"You can't stop the waves, but you can learn to surf."
–JON KABAT-ZINN

AS I WAS IN THE PROCESS OF WRITING THIS
book, I reached out to my former team of eight district man-
agers and asked each of them what their favorite team-build
activity had been when we worked together. The overwhelming
winner was when I had coordinated a meeting and then a team-
build activity at the beach. I had initially hesitated to include this

activity in this book because it felt so simple, but because of the tremendous feedback they shared, I just couldn't leave it out.

Recently, I saw a piece of advice posted on social media. It said that if you are writing a book, you should be reading a lot, so that you can tap into your inspiration and creativity. I was sitting on a plane to Colorado and decided to crack open Brené Brown's *Dare to Lead.* I had been reading it while I was at my prior job and had not finished it. At this time, I had been on hiatus for a little over three months, and for those first three months, the thought of looking at another leadership book was not appealing to me at all. I was detoxing and taking a break. But on that flight, I opened the book again, and BAM! Right there in the middle of the book, the Universe gave me the answer as to why this very simple team build had been so impactful to my crew. She referenced an article in the *Harvard Business Review* that was about companies that reported high levels of exhaustion. A research team had examined what was driving these high levels of exhaustion, and they discovered that the employees were not exhausted from their workloads per se but because they were lonely. The loneliness was causing the exhaustion. I immediately searched for the article and found it: "America's Loneliest Workers, According to Research." I was excited when I saw that one of the contributing authors of the article was Shawn Achor, author of *The Happiness Project.*

I had a lightbulb moment on the plane. "This is why!" I realized. This is why my employees felt our beach bonfire was so impactful to them. Because they were exhausted and felt lonely. It was an exercise that brought all of them together in one space and caused them to view each other with empathy and not just as a coworker they have to put up with, compete with, or, for that matter, step over on their way to the top. The research from the article showed that "loneliness threatens not only our physical health and well-being, but also our livelihood." It also provided evidence that loneliness has the same effect as fifteen cigarettes a day in terms of health-care outcomes and health-care costs. Yet we are often blind to this hidden drain on health and revenue. "Lonelier workers perform more poorly, quit more often, and feel less satisfied with their jobs—costing employers upwards of $3.5 billion in the U.S. alone." It was discovered that one of the biggest amplifiers to help alleviate loneliness was for leaders to assist individuals in having shared meaning and collective wins in a supportive work environment. The article also made sure to counsel leaders to look for signs of loneliness such as social withdrawal and diminished mood.

I had called this meeting and required everyone to attend

in person because I recognized that my team needed some fun and a break. I booked us a hotel on the beach in Monterey, California, and offered up the ocean-view rooms to the top performers of the week so they had something to look forward to.

Here is how you can replicate the "S'mores and More Beach Bonfire":

If you have the budget, have the hotel set it up for you. We had a firepit, tiki torches and an entire bar cart full of drinks and S'mores kits ready for us.

On another occasion, I purchased all the materials myself, and we had a lot of fun setting up the scene together. After our meeting, I took everyone to a nice dinner to ensure they were well-fed so no one was "hangry." Then, everyone gathered at the beach for roasting S'mores and enjoying camaraderie around the firepit. And, okay, maybe there was a cocktail or two that was consumed. Ha-ha!

Here is the most important part of this activity: I required that each individual bring their favorite quote or inspirational message to share with the group around the fire. I kicked off the event by reading a motivational passage about the ocean. Then we went around to each individual who had brought their favorite inspirational message, and they had an opportunity to share it and talk about the reason why it was so impactful to them. The fact that each person was able to share what meant most to them and why, with several active listeners, is the reason this worked towards alleviating their loneliness. Each person felt seen and heard; for that time at the beach, they felt as if they mattered. It was an amazing experience and one that I will never forget, and, clearly, my team has never forgotten either.

If you aren't near a beach, you could do the same exercise with a firepit at someone's home or at a campsite or park. Just make sure that you get everyone together in person, if you can, and have them participate in this shared bonding experience. If you are a leader of many individuals and you are geographically challenged, I encourage you to try this in a virtual, dedicated team meeting over the phone or through video conference. It will still be impactful by helping to reduce that loneliness factor. The deep connection and openness which occurs by just offering the space to share will be dramatically impactful to all involved.

I like to think of this team build as one of those amazing recipes that chefs cook in which there are only a few simple ingredients, and yet it tastes phenomenal! You will never forget the meal because it was so uncomplicated and cooked to perfection.

MISCELLANEOUS MODALITIES/ TEAM-BUILD ACTIVITY IDEAS

"Pay attention to what has heart and meaning."
–THE FOUR-FOLD WAY,
ANGELES ARRIEN

MAKE TIME FOR TEA

Drinking tea is such a beautiful ritual that connects humans with each other and is practiced in many cultures all over the world. For one hour (or whatever length of time works for you) gather your team and just sit, drink tea and be. It is nice if everyone is drinking the same kind of tea from the same pot. No cell phones, no music, just focus on the slow drinking of the tea and connecting with each other.

You can add to this exercise by setting up the space with pillows or blankets for each individual to sit on. Scattered candles or plants will add to the ambience. You might want to start the session by passing a burning palo santo or sage stick around and asking each individual to set a positive intention for what they would like to bring into their lives as they ingest their tea with the group.

Provide tea cups with unique symbols or quotes on them. As you drink the tea, ask each person to describe the cup they chose, and to reflect on why they chose that one. You can also use prompt cards or coaching questions. Have each person draw a question from the deck and reflect on the answer with the group. (I've highlighted my favorite types on the Resources page.)

Make it special, make the time and stop scrolling and running off to the next task for just a while. Side note: This could be done as a wine-tasting team-build activity as well.

RESTORATIVE YOGA SESSIONS

Have a trained yoga instructor do a private session for you and your team. If you do a restorative session it is very low impact so most everyone will be able to participate without any risk of injury. This can be done by most yoga instructors at a very reasonable price and coordinated for an hour. At the end have the instructor lead a guided visualization on sending positive energy to people in the world. If they have sound healing bowls this is a great time to incorporate that stress-reducing technique into this practice.

QUICK WAYS TO MAKE AN IMPACT

"You never know when a moment and a few sincere words can have an impact on a life."
–ZIG ZIGLAR

CREATE APPRECIATION ANCHORS

A huge part of emotional intelligence is having an emotional management strategy. One of the ways to help facilitate this is to have an appreciation anchor. According to the Institute for Health and Human Potential, the brain cannot experience fear and appreciation at the same time. Appreciation releases counter chemistry, which increases perspective, energy and complex thought. An appreciation anchor pushes back on our negativity bias.

In the past, I have created appreciation anchors for many different events with employees and teams; crystal pouches are one of my favorites. I typically consult with a crystal master for the best combination to create the energy and feeling I am trying to bring into the meeting, conference or space. For example, for one national conference I created a "Positivity Pouch" which contained smoky quartz, amethyst, yellow citrine and pyrite. This combination was meant to help keep people grounded, guard against negativity and increase productivity. I put the crystals in tiny pouches with little labels and handed them out at the conference. People love receiving positive anchors like that.

I also use crystals as anchors for leaders/coaches when they have a public speaking engagement. Anytime someone has to present in front of an audience it is always a good stress and anxiety reducer to have a couple of small crystals in your pocket as an emotional intelligence anchor. I used this strategy every time I would speak in front of large audiences and when I was paired with a partner on presentations, I would always give that person one or two to carry as well. This gesture resonates very strongly with people. Years later, I still receive picture messages from leaders who are holding crystals that they'll put in their pockets before going on stage to present. You can tie appreciation anchors into your company's vision and/or mission for a great tangible item that will remind your employees of your culture.

Other great appreciation anchors include stress-reducing pamphlets, books, or daily affirmation calendars that have quotes/tips for relaxation or instructions on how to breathe and center oneself. (See my Resources Page)

POSITIVE AFFIRMATION CARDS

Put together a bowl of cards with inspirational affirmations or quotes listed on each one. Packs of these are available online or see my Resources page. At the end of your meeting or session, have each person close their eyes and take a deep, centering breath. Have them reach into the bowl with their eyes closed and pull out a life affirmation quote that is meant just for them. If they would like, they can read the message they received to their peers and share their thoughts. Let them keep the card as a reminder of the message they received. This is such a quick, impactful way to end a meeting and leave everyone in a positive, inspired mindset. People seem to just get what was meant for them and I am still contacted years later with pictures from individuals who still have their cards.

EXPRESSIONS OF GRATITUDE

"Grateful people sleep better. Gratitude improves self-esteem. Gratitude enhances empathy and reduces aggression."

–FROM "7 SCIENTIFICALLY PROVEN BENEFITS OF GRATITUDE THAT WILL MOTIVATE YOU TO GIVE THANKS YEAR-ROUND" BY AMY MORIN, FORBES

A great way to kick off a meeting with a group or an individual is to start by sharing what they are grateful for. Start your sessions off with each individual reporting back on what they are grateful for that day, week or month. They can choose something related to business or their personal life to help create a connection with the overall group.

MEETING ENVIRONMENTS

For in-person meetings, make sure you arrive early to set up the room. Bring an essential oil diffuser and put some lavender, which raises positive vibrations, or a balancing blend into it. This will set the tone in the room. Make sure that you have snacks and drinks readily available as well. If individuals are stressed out or hungry, their brains may not be open to creativity and possibility. The goal is to make your employees as comfortable as possible so their creativity and inspiration can shine through in the meeting.

WITH GRATITUDE

I am hoping that after reading all of these different activities and modalities your creativity is flowing and you try each one in your own way. Whether it is with a group of people, co-workers, a coachee, friends, or family members, these activities can be translated throughout all parts of your life to help foster human connection and bring back into our lives the qualities that make us human, such as our ability to love, have compassion, and be creative.

When I was born into this world
The only things I knew were to love, laugh, and
shine my light brightly.
Then as I grew, people told me to stop laughing.
"Take life seriously," they said,
"If you want to get ahead in this world."
So I stopped laughing.
People told me, "Be careful who you love
If you don't want your heart broken."
So I stopped loving.
They said, "Don't shine your light so bright
As it draws too much attention onto you."
So I stopped shining
And became small
And withered
And died
Only to learn upon death
That all that matters in life
Is to love, laugh, and shine our light brightly!
--ANITA MOORJANI

RESOURCES

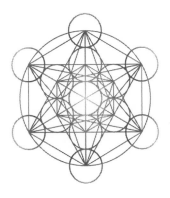

Pamphlet: How to Relax by Thich Nhat Hanh

    Journal Prompt Cards: Mood Lady cards from

    Valentino Coaching

Question Prompt Cards: "What's Your Word?"

    MyIntent.org

Essential oils: Doterra

Flying Wish Paper: Amazon

    Affirmation/Inspirational cards: "Power

    Thought Cards" by Lousie Hay, "I Can Do It"

    Cards by

    Louise Hay

Daily Affirmation Calendar: "I Can Do It"

by Louise Hay

    Tea Mugs: zpots.com

NOTES